STORIES

OF THE

POETS

SUZI MEE

Design by Marijka Kostiw

Earlier versions of some essays in this book were published in *Harvard* Magazine and *Literary Cavalcade*.

Credits for photographs of the poets appear on page 112.

ACKNOWLEDGMENTS

Grateful acknowledgment is made to the following publisher for the use of copyrighted material. Every effort has been made to obtain permission to use previously published material. Any errors or omissions are unintentional. University of Pittsburgh Press for "Station" by Sharon Olds. Reprinted from SATAN SAYS, by Sharon Olds, by permission of the University of Pittsburgh Press. Copyright © 1980 by Sharon Olds.

ISBN 0-590-35584-8

12 11 10 9 8 7 6 5 4 3 2   1 2 3/9
                                              31

CONTENTS

To Erin and Charles, both poets

FOREWORD

Students often ask me, "How does someone become a poet?" "How does a poet live?" "There are so many poets, which ones should I pay attention to?" This book is an attempt to answer these questions.

Each essay is the "story" of a particular poet and his or her work. It is the story of language and images, of individuality and kinship with other people. But mostly, it is the story of a man or woman straining toward the outer reaches of the mind.

I hope these stories will help lead you to your own "outer reaches."

Suzi Mee
New York
July 1989

William Blake

THE VISIONARY WORLD OF WILLIAM BLAKE (1757-1827)

The English poet William Blake lived in two worlds: the visible world of everyday life in London and the invisible world of the spirit. His first recorded vision occurred at age four, when he screamed that God's face was staring at him through the window. Once he almost received a beating for telling his father that he had seen a tree full of angels. But eventually his parents came to accept the unusual imagination of their second son. Instead of sending him to school, they allowed him to study at home under his mother's tutelage.

At the age of ten he was enrolled at a drawing school, where he spent much of his time sketching people and animals. He also visited art collections to copy prints. Then, at fourteen, he was apprenticed for seven years to a master engraver who sent him to Westminster Abbey to make drawings of the sculptures and Gothic ornamentation. While there, Blake witnessed a rare event: the opening of the tomb of King Edward I, who had died in 1307. The sight of this perfectly preserved figure from more than four centuries earlier—dressed in a richly jeweled robe of red damask lined with satin and cloth of gold—dazzled the young boy and confirmed his feeling that the past, present, and future were all one. The vivid reds and golds would reappear later not only in his paintings but also in his poems.

Between the ages of twelve and twenty, Blake composed fragments of poems that eventually would be published as *Poetical Sketches*. In many of these early lines, a painterly eye is already apparent:

> ...speak silence with thy glimmering eyes,
> And wash the dusk with silver.

In 1782, Blake met a kindhearted though illiterate country girl named Catherine Boucher. According to contemporary reports, Catherine instantly recognized Blake as her future husband and fainted with emotion. Sympathetic to visionary experiences, she was the perfect companion for Blake. She understood when he wrote,

> Now I a fourfold vision see,
> And a fourfold vision is given to me...

Blake's fourfold vision consisted of: (1) single vision, or seeing only through the eyes; (2) seeing through the eyes plus the additional perception of the mind; (3) the first two plus the emotions; (4) the first three plus mystical ecstasy.

Catherine called Blake her "master" and his welfare always came first. She served as friend, housekeeper, cook, and engraving assistant all in one. Childless, she and Blake both considered works of art to be their "children," especially the *Songs of Innocence*, which Blake completed in 1789. These poems, illustrated by original drawings, were written "for children of all ages with innocent hearts... Innocence dwells with Wisdom, but never with Ignorance," Blake noted.

> Little Lamb, who made thee?
> Dost thou know who made thee?
> Gave thee life & bid thee feed,
> By the stream & o'er the mead;

Gave thee clothing of delight,
Softest clothing, wooly bright;
Gave thee such a tender voice,
Making all the vales rejoice!
　Little Lamb, who made thee?
　Dost thou know who made thee?

But the world of innocence also had its sorrows. Living in London, where children as young as six years worked as chimney sweeps or bootblacks, Blake was painfully aware of the exploitation of innocence and noted it in a sequel, *Songs of Experience*.

I wander thro' each charter'd street,
Near where the charter'd Thames does flow,
And mark in every face I meet
Marks of weakness, marks of woe.
　　　. . .
How the Chimney-sweeper's cry
Every black'ning Church appalls;
And the hapless Soldier's sigh
Runs in blood down Palace walls.

In *Songs of Experience*, Blake further examined the theme of innocence versus evil. Sometimes evil possesses a powerful beauty:

Tyger! Tyger! burning bright
In the forests of the night,
What immortal hand or eye
Could frame thy fearful symmetry?
　　　. . .
When the stars threw down their spears,
And water'd heaven with their tears,
Did he smile his work to see?
Did he who made the Lamb make thee?

Ever optimistic, Blake felt certain that his books would eventually lift him out of poverty. But his vision was too odd for the general public. Friends tried to help by introducing him to would-be patrons, but sooner or later his independent spirit would assert itself and undermine the relationship. One of these patrons, the well-to-do poet William Hayley, enticed the Blakes to move to the country, where he installed them in a small cottage on his estate. But Blake felt cramped in such surroundings, and eventually they went back to London.

After their return, material conditions worsened for the Blakes, although the visions multiplied: sometimes it was the heads of historical figures that Blake saw, and sometimes it was the terrifying "ghost of a flea." But such "visitors" brought no food to the table. Often Mrs. Blake would put out two empty plates in order to remind her distracted husband of the seriousness of their plight.

After Blake died, his reputation slowly spread among a few artists. Such notable poets as William Wordsworth and Samuel Taylor Coleridge praised his work. With the appearance in prominent London journals of several critical essays about his work, Blake's visions came to be regarded as evidence of the vast, and often unexplored, potential of the human mind. The visions, and the images resulting from them, have perhaps inspired more contemporary poets than any other single literary phenomenon.

WILLIAM WORDSWORTH'S INFLUENCE
ON MODERN POETRY (1770–1850)

In 1798, when he was twenty-eight, William
Wordsworth set out on a trip to Germany in the company
of his sister Dorothy and his friend Samuel Taylor
Coleridge. To help pay for the journey, Wordsworth and
Coleridge had put together a joint volume of poetry, *Lyrical Ballads*. The book included Coleridge's *The Rime of
the Ancient Mariner* and Wordsworth's early experiments
in using everyday language in poems. Before this book
appeared, the vocabulary used in most English poetry was
formal and consciously "poetic."

The idea for the trip apparently originated with
Coleridge, who wanted to learn German. To pursue this
aim, he separated from the Wordsworths after several
weeks and went his own way. The Wordsworths,
meanwhile, settled in the medieval town of Goslar at the
foot of the Hartz Mountains.

Since neither Dorothy nor William spoke German, they
felt cut off from the people around them. Also it was bitterly
cold. Huddling in front of the fire, they spent most of their
time reading, writing, and reflecting on the past.
Increasingly, Wordsworth began to recall the pleasures of
his youth spent among valleys and lakes, woods and
streams. He had long been searching for a theme that would

allow him a scope comparable to those of the great epics: Homer's *Odyssey*, Dante's *Divine Comedy*, and Milton's *Paradise Lost*. In Goslar, such a theme came to him.

Like the subjects of many earlier epics, it involved a quest, a search. The difference was that Wordsworth's quest would explore the past. Its goal would be a search into the relationship between the mind and its surroundings, particularly natural surroundings. Wordsworth wished to know how trees, flowers, rivers, rocks, and rain affected thoughts and ideas, how they created delicate moods as well as vague dreams of the future.

In remembering his past, Wordsworth hoped to evoke a time when "the common face of Nature spake to me Rememberable things..." His tools for the search — memory, observation, insight, and imagination — are every poet's tools, but in Wordsworth's case, they were sharpened by ambition.

When he and his sister returned to England, they settled in Grasmere, a village nestled among the mountains in the Lake District. Here he began working on his epic in earnest, and the work gradually evolved into fourteen books, or chapters, each describing a stage of Wordsworth's life.

Books I and II are devoted to memories of childhood, when he would stand

> Beneath some rock, listening to notes that are
> The ghostly language of the ancient earth,
> Or make their dim abode in distant winds.
> Thence did I drink the visionary power;
> And deem not profitless those fleeting moods
> Of shadowy exultation...

He describes rowing along streams overhung with trees, running through meadows "like a galloping steed," climbing tall rocks, eating strawberries with fresh cream, bathing under waterfalls, ice-skating "all shod with steel."

Books III and IV concern his college days at Cambridge University. This was a period of stretching his mind by studying the great philosophers, historians, scientists, and poets. Among the authors he read was the Spanish novelist Cervantes, whose *Don Quixote* inspired a dream that stands at the heart of Wordsworth's epic poem. In the dream, an Arab nomad appears before him holding a stone in one hand and a shell in the other. Both objects are "books" in which one can read the world. The stone represents the world's formation and history, while the shell has

> Voices more than all the winds, with power
> To exhilarate the spirit, and to soothe,
> Through every clime, the heart of human kind...

These voices symbolize the inspiration that often comes to those who are close to nature.

After a stay in London (Books VII and VIII), where Wordsworth confronts humankind in all its infinite variety, and a stay in France (Book IX), where he hears the rumblings of the French Revolution, he returns to the English countryside. Here, amid the natural surroundings that he has begun to think of as "holy ground," he hears "the language of the heavens." To him, these are signs that he has been "called" to be a poet. With this discovery, the epic has come full circle. Wordsworth titled his autobiographical poem *The Prelude*.

The nature philosophy underlining *The Prelude* would be later echoed by contemporary American poets such as James Wright and Robert Bly. These poets seek, as Wordsworth did, to unite the "truth without" with the "truth within," thereby achieving a fresh and luminous vision of the world around them.

Walt Whitman [signature]

WALT WHITMAN AND THE BEGINNINGS
OF AMERICAN POETRY (1819–1892)

The United States declared its political independence from England in 1776, but its poetic independence was not achieved until 1855. In that year an obscure American journalist published a poem called "There Was a Child Went Forth." The poem was written in free verse, or verse with no fixed meter or rhyme scheme. Its lines stretched across the page like America stretching from ocean to ocean:

> There was a child went forth every day,
> And the first object he look'd upon, that object he became,
> And that object became part of him for the day or a certain
>   part of the day,
> Or for many years or stretching cycles of years...

The author of this poem, Walt Whitman, was born in Long Island, New York, "within a stone's throw of the sea." His father was a farmer-carpenter who had a difficult time making ends meet. There was little privacy in the tiny Whitman house, and barely enough food on the table. Yet from these dreary surroundings emerged a figure who would exult in the "rush of the streets," in the play of sunlight on grass and trees, in physical health, in the simple fact of being alive.

The change of young Walter—a child very dependent on his mother—into the poet Walt Whitman did not occur overnight. It was a slow process that probably began with Whitman's apprenticeship, at age twelve, to a typesetter in Brooklyn. The act of setting type by hand made language—words, punctuation, and sentence length—concrete, vital. When his apprenticeship was completed four years later, he first worked for a time as a journeyman printer and then took a job as a country schoolteacher on Long Island. Although he enjoyed teaching, he often had to cope with the most wretched conditions in small, ill-heated schoolhouses.

In 1841 Whitman moved to New York City and, as a free-lance reporter for several minor newspapers, absorbed what he called "the fascinating chaos" of street life. He attended political rallies—sometimes making speeches himself—and became a familiar figure in the smoke-filled rooms along lower Broadway. When he began to speak out against slavery, more than one newspaper refused to print his columns.

The turning point of Whitman's literary development came in 1842, when he heard a lecture by Ralph Waldo Emerson, who was at that time the most eminent man of letters in America. In this lecture, Emerson defined the characteristics of the ideal American poet: "He visits without fear the factory, the railroad, and the wharf. When he lifts his great voice, men gather to him... and immediately the tools of their bench, and the riches of their useful arts... seem to them weapons of romance... "

Sitting in the audience, Whitman felt that Emerson was speaking directly to him. But how was he to forge the new American verse? How was he to give poetic form to such a vast and untamed landscape? And what should replace iambic pentameter, the five-stress line that American poets had traditionally used? It took Whitman thirteen more years to find an answer, which came from childhood influences and his surroundings. His "new poem," when it emerged, contained long, freely flowing lines, with a rhythm similar to the ebb and flow of the sea, and a democratic outlook embracing young, old, black, white, man, woman, rich, poor, ignorant, educated. This poem, published in 1855 shortly after "There Was a Child Went Forth," was called *Leaves of Grass*. It bears the unmistakable stamp of Whitman's robust self-confidence:

> I celebrate myself, and sing myself,
> And what I assume you shall assume,
> For every atom belonging to me as good belongs to you...

During his long lifetime, Walt Whitman produced several other "master" poems, notably "Out of the Cradle Endlessly Rocking" and "When Lilacs Last in the Dooryard Bloom'd," an elegy on the death of President Abraham Lincoln. But it was *Leaves of Grass* that broke with literary tradition and set American poetry off in a new direction.

THE RIDDLE OF EMILY DICKINSON
(1830–1886)

During the latter part of her life, Emily Dickinson wrote on a scrap of paper:

> The riddle we can guess
> We speedily despise—
> Not anything is stale so long
> As yesterday's surprise—

The idea of the riddle and riddle-making—which she sometimes called "telling it 'slant'"—pervaded both Dickinson's life and her art.

Emily Dickinson grew up in a household that was dominated by her father, a prominent lawyer in Amherst, Massachusetts, and treasurer of Amherst College. Young Emily developed a talent for sidestepping her father's many rules, and that talent may have contributed to her lifelong tendency toward secrecy. "Father is too busy with his Briefs," she wrote, "to notice what we do." In contrast, her mother was a shadowy presence. Emily said of her, "My mother does not care for thought," and left it at that.

Emily *did* care for thought, but she had trouble explaining her thoughts to others. Her remarks often bewildered her beloved older brother, Austin, and her younger sister, Lavinia. "...if we had come up for the first time from two wells, her [Vinnie's] astonishment would not be greater at some of the things I say," Emily remarked. She herself enjoyed the "wiles of Words." "What a beautiful Word 'Waters' is," she once exclaimed to a friend. Yet words also held the power to wound and injure. "She dealt her pretty words like Blades," one poem states. Such power had to be deflected, diverted, in the same way that a surging river must be diverted into calm streams. Riddles were Emily's streams.

> Tell all the truth but tell it slant—
> Success in circuit lies;
> Too bright for our infirm delight
> The truth's superb surprise...

After attending Amherst Academy, Emily Dickinson went away from home (for the first and only time) to the Mount Holyoke Female Seminary in nearby South Hadley. In later years a school friend recalled her: "Her eyes were a lovely auburn, soft and warm, her hair lay in rings of the same color all over her head, and her skin and teeth were fine. She had a demure manner which brightened easily into fun where she felt at home, but among strangers she was rather shy, silent... She was exquisitely neat and careful in her dress, and always had flowers about her. She was one of the wits of the school, and there were no signs in her life and character of the future recluse."

Returning home, she gardened and baked bread. But increasingly she remained in her upstairs room, composing her brief, mysterious messages to the world—or to herself.

> I'm ceded—I've stopped being theirs—
> The name they dropped upon my face
> With water, in the country church
> Is finished using, now,
> And they can put it with my dolls,
> My childhood, and the string of spools,
> I've finished threading—too—

These years were marked by events that most people would consider insignificant: the blooming of the yellow sunflowers in spring, autumn sunsets, a parade glimpsed briefly from a downstairs window. More and more her poems—written in a thin, spidery script that was as hard to decipher as the content—concentrated on personal feelings. Sometimes they were joyful:

> I cannot dance upon my toes—
> No man instructed me—
> But oftentimes, among my mind,
> A glee possesseth me...

Sometimes they were sad:

> There's a certain slant of light,
> On winter afternoons—
> That oppresses, like the weight
> Of cathedral tunes—

Although Emily Dickinson claimed not to care about being published, this was not quite true. In 1862, she wrote to a stranger, the Reverend Thomas Wentworth Higginson, whose literary essays she had admired in the *Atlantic Monthly*: "Are you too deeply occupied to say if my verse is alive?" Enclosed were four poems. Their eccentric punctuation and rhymes left Mr. Higginson at a loss about how to respond. At last he wrote back with suggestions for improvements, and a few questions. The improvements were ignored altogether, and the questions evaded with answers like "You asked how old I was? I made no verse, but one or two, until this winter, sir." Such coyness served to stimulate Higginson's curiosity and the two continued to correspond, off and on, until Emily's death. But he never urged her to publish.

In 1874 her father died. "His heart was pure and terrible," Emily wrote to a friend, "and I think no other like it exists." After her mother's death, she and Vinnie lived alone—"like friendly and absolute monarchs, each in his own domain"—in the big house. Her life was as austere and solitary as that of a nun in a religious order; her religion was poetry. "If I read a book and it makes my whole body so cold no fire can ever warm me, I know that is poetry. If I feel physically as if the top of my head were taken off, I know that is poetry. These are the only ways I know it. Is there any other way?"

During her lifetime, Emily Dickinson wrote 1,775 poems, which were found after her death in neat packets tied with ribbons. A neighbor, Mabel Loomis Todd, together with the Reverend Mr. Higginson, selected 116 of the poems and took them to a Boston publisher. Grudgingly, he finally agreed to put out a small volume. Much to everyone's amazement, the book received glowing reviews. One critic called it "a new species of art."

WILLIAM BUTLER YEATS: THE YOUNG MUSE (1865–1939)

Upon accepting the Nobel Prize for Literature in 1923, W. B. Yeats observed that when he was young, his Muse was old, but as he grew older, his Muse grew younger. He was not exaggerating. Yeats was among the relatively few major poets who did their best work in old age. When he died at the age of seventy-four, the *New Republic* could state without a trace of irony: "He died, like Shelley, at the height of his powers and with half his work unwritten." (Percy Bysshe Shelley, the English Romantic poet, died in a sailing accident when he was only thirty.)

Born in a suburb of Dublin, Ireland, Yeats spent much of his childhood in the county of Sligo with his grandparents. The Sligo countryside, with its folklore and tales of the supernatural, made a lasting impression. Though his goal was to be a painter like his father, he soon discovered that his true talent lay in painting images with words rather than with brushes.

When his parents moved to London in 1887, Yeats went with them. His first book of poems, *The Wanderings of Oisin*, was a minor success. According to a contemporary report, the young Yeats was "very pale, exceedingly thin, a raven lock over his forehead, his face so narrow that there was hardly room in it for his luminous black eyes."

He also affected a green cape and dabbled in the occult. The visionary early Romantic William Blake was his poetic master. Though much of Yeats's youthful poetry lacked solidity, every now and then one could detect touches of brilliance.

> I will arise and go now, and go to Innisfree,
> And a small cabin build there, of clay and wattles made...

Returning to Ireland in 1896, he met the fiery Irish actress and patriot Maud Gonne, and was captivated for life. "I had never thought to see in a living woman such great beauty. It belonged to famous pictures, to poetry, to some legendary past..."

He wrote a play, *Cathleen ni Houlihan*, in which Maud Gonne played the part of a heroine who exhorts people to fight for Irish freedom. The play created a tremendous stir, causing one critic to comment, "The effect of *Cathleen ni Houlihan* on me was that I went home asking myself if such plays should be produced unless one was prepared for people to go out and be shot."

Yeats himself had doubts about militant patriotism. Yet later, after the Easter Rebellion of 1916, when rebels tried to seize control of Ireland from British hands, he wrote a moving tribute to the martyred leaders:

> I write it out in a verse—
> MacDonagh and MacBride
> And Connolly and Pearse
> Now and in time to be,
> Wherever green is worn,
> Are changed, changed utterly:
> A terrible beauty is born.

But Yeats's personal relationship with Maud Gonne proved a frustration. For months he pleaded with her to marry him, but she refused, calling him (a bit condescendingly) "Silly Willie." Yeats was miserable. He

described this period as the most wretched of his whole life.

Fortunately, a friend came to his rescue: Lady Augusta Gregory. Herself a gifted writer, Lady Gregory recognized Yeats's talent and determined to help him. Not only did he become a frequent guest at her estate, Coole Park, but she joined him in starting a national Irish theater, later called the Abbey. With her encouragement, Yeats began to write plays in earnest.

The next important influence in Yeats's life came in the person of Ezra Pound. Under Pound's critical eye, a marked change occurred in Yeats's writing. Losing the soft, mystical quality that had marred much of his earlier work, his poetry grew more concrete and immediate. With Pound serving as his best man, Yeats married Georgie Hyde-Lees in 1917. Despite the difference in their ages—Yeats was fifty-two, Georgie much younger—it seems to have been a happy marriage. Yeats reported to Lady Gregory that his wife "was kind, wise, and unselfish." If the poetry is any evidence, the union released latent powers that coincided with the aftermath of World War I:

> Things fall apart; the center cannot hold;
> Mere anarchy is loosed upon the world...

The couple settled in a Norman tower in Thoor Ballylee, near Lady Gregory's home, which Yeats christened with these lines:

> I, the poet William Yeats,
> With old mill boards and sea-green slates,
> And smith work from the Fort forge,
> Restored this tower for my wife George...

After the birth of his two children, a son and a daughter (and after winning the Nobel Prize), Yeats embarked upon his most creative period. Yet it brought a touch of bitterness: old age was also beckoning.

> An aged man is but a paltry thing,
> A tattered coat upon a stick, unless...

How to cope with a young Muse tapping an old man's shoulder? This was Yeats's dilemma. He solved it (somewhat) by evoking an imagination born of craft and knowledge, such as the sages of ancient Byzantium once possessed.

> ...unless
> Soul clap its hands and sing, and louder sing
> For every tatter in its mortal dress,
> Nor is there singing school but studying
> Monuments of its own magnificence;
> And therefore I have sailed the seas and come
> To the holy city of Byzantium.
>
> (*from* "Sailing to Byzantium")

The contemporary Irish poet Seamus Heaney (see page 99) has described Yeats's legacy:

"What Yeats offers the practising writer is an example of labour, perseverance... He reminds you that revision and slog-work are what you may have to undergo if you seek the satisfactions of...inspiration."

Thanks to the young Muse (perhaps, in part, his wife), a phoenix rose out of the ashes of Yeats's "slog-work." Toward the end of his life, he joined the ranks of those few who "had changed their throats and had the throats of birds."

Robert Frost

ROBERT FROST: PUBLIC POET AND PRIVATE MAN (1874–1963)

In 1961, at John F. Kennedy's presidential inauguration, Robert Frost stood up to read a poem composed especially for the occasion. The sun beamed down on his white thatch of hair and also on the page he was holding, making it impossible for him to see the words clearly. Waving Vice President Lyndon Johnson aside—Johnson tried to shield the page from the glare with his top hat—Frost stopped reading and proceeded to recite from memory an earlier poem that turned out to be even more fitting than the first:

> The land was ours before we were the land's.
> She was our land more than a hundred years
> Before we were her people. She was ours
> In Massachusetts, in Virginia,
> But we were English, still colonials,
> Possessing what we still were unpossessed by,
> Possessed by what we now no more possessed...

The crowd gave him a thunderous ovation. Newspapers and television reporters declared him America's unofficial poet laureate. For Frost, it was the climax of a lifetime of public appearances, which had begun over sixty years earlier at his high school graduation.

Robert Frost (or "Rob," as he was called) had made

such consistently superior grades in high school in Lawrence, Massachusetts, that even before the final tally was in, the principal had declared him valedictorian of his graduating class. But after the last round of exams, another student (and secret poet), Elinor White, was found to be a few grade points ahead. The principal finally declared *both* of them valedictorians. At the graduation ceremony, Frost, who had already determined to be a poet himself, was stricken with nervousness during Elinor's speech. He dashed off the platform, returning just in time to deliver his own address on the subject of Wordsworth. He gave his address so smoothly that those listening had no idea of the sensitive nature lurking behind the boyish mask.

Some of Frost's sensitivities probably resulted from his childhood years. At an early age, his parents separated, and Frost and his sister were often shunted around from relative to relative and friend to friend while their mother sought a teaching position. At long last the parents resolved their difficulties, but by that time, his father was in frail health and soon died of tuberculosis. To support the family, his mother started a school in Lawrence. As he grew older, Frost would fill in whenever she was sick or needed an extra hand.

After graduation, Frost entered Dartmouth College but, impatient with formal schooling, left after a few months. He had also fallen deeply in love with Elinor White and kept begging her to quit college and marry him. After obtaining her college degree, she finally relented, even agreeing to Frost's condition that he should be the only poet in the family. Although she would often criticize her husband's poetry and offer suggestions for improvement, she herself never wrote another line.

Frost was fond of saying that three occupations would engage him all of his life: teaching, farming, and poetry. This statement was true to an extent, though there was

never any doubt that poetry came first. Whenever the other two became too demanding, he would quit whatever he was doing and seek out a place where he might be able to write. This pattern started early, when he took a job teaching at his mother's school and then left after several years to try his hand at poultry farming. But neither he nor Elinor had the stamina for such hard labor, and the venture was not a success.

Around the same time, their first child, a son, died, leaving both parents in a state of despondency. In an effort to assist the young couple, Frost's paternal grandfather purchased a farm for them in Derry, New Hampshire. It was in Derry that the other four Frost children were born. It was also in Derry that Frost became particularly attentive to the farm life around him—the changing of seasons, chores, conversations with neighbors, the loneliness of farm wives—subjects that would appear in some of his best poems.

> You come to fetch me from my work tonight
> When supper's on the table, and we'll see
> If I can leave off burying the white
> Soft petals fallen from the apple tree
> (Soft petals, yes, but not so barren quite,
> Mingled with these, smooth bean and wrinkled pea;)
> And go along with you ere you lose sight
> Of what you came for and become like me,
> Slave to a springtime passion for the earth...

After several years of farming (and intermittently having poems rejected for publication), Frost grew restless and sought a teaching position in nearby Pinkerton Academy. This lasted until 1912 when, tired of being an obscure poet, he took the biggest risk of his life. He decided to sell the Derry farm and gamble everything on a trip to England, where he hoped to sell his first book of poetry, *A Boy's Will.*

After landing in Plymouth, England, the family settled

in rural Beaconsfield. Within two months, Frost took the completed manuscript of *A Boy's Will* to a London publisher, who, to Frost's astonished delight, soon accepted it for publication. Encouraged by this success, he began to familiarize himself with the British literary scene. He called on Ezra Pound, but was put off by Pound's attempts to edit some of Frost's poems. He met William Butler Yeats, whom he admired—though from a distance. Frost's closest alliances were with lesser-known figures, such as the critic Edward Thomas and the poet Robert Bridges.

When copies of *A Boy's Will* finally appeared, Frost sent them to literary acquaintances in America and, through letters, subtly coached them on how the book should be reviewed. Returning to the United States and to a farm in Franconia, New Hampshire, Frost found that he had acquired a small but substantial reputation, which widened after *A Boy's Will* was published in America. Gradually he began to receive invitations to read his poetry at various colleges and literary forums. Figures such as Amy Lowell, who had ignored him before, now asked him to dinner. Although Frost enjoyed these gestures of acceptance, a part of him still rankled from the long period of neglect. He took a teaching job at Amherst College and then quit in a burst of resentment. And he raged about the "summer people" who dropped by the farm in Franconia. As a result of such intrusions, the Frost family moved once more, this time to South Shaftsbury, Vermont.

In the next few years, three new volumes of poetry appeared and two of them, *Collected Poems* in 1931 and *A Further Range* in 1937, won Pulitzer Prizes. Frost traveled all over the country, presenting to his public the picture of a genial poet who delivers homespun anecdotes about country life. Yet there were dark aspects that foreshadowed events to come. In 1938, his turbulent marriage ended with the death of his wife. In 1940, his only son, who had long suffered from acute emotional problems, took his own life.

Frost, with his mercurial temperament, felt partly responsible for both of these tragedies. After a long fit of depression, however, his sense of survival emerged and he determined to bury his grief and "carry on." In his last few years—perhaps in an effort to stave off loneliness—his pace became even more frantic. He gave lectures and readings, and represented the State Department in a number of trips abroad. Awards and honors were heaped upon him, among them a special Congressional Medal, which was presented on his eighty-eighth birthday.

Robert Frost was a polished craftsman who believed strongly in the fusion between what a poem tried to say and how the poet tried to make the poem say it. "Style," he said, "is the way [a writer] carries himself toward his ideas and deeds." And to an old friend he wrote, "A poem...begins as a lump in the throat, a sense of wrong, a homesickness, a lovesickness... It finds the thought and the thought finds the words."

Carl Sandburg

CARL SANDBURG: POET OF THE PEOPLE
(1878–1967)

Carl Sandburg was born in Galesburg, a town in western Illinois whose main street opened onto the prairie. His father, an illiterate Swedish immigrant, became a blacksmith who helped forge train railings for the vast network then being extended from one end of the continent to the other. Some of the blacksmith's muscle and sweat would later seep into Sandburg's poetry:

> Lay me on an anvil, O God.
> Beat me and hammer me into a steel spike...

as would the wheat and red clover and corn of the plains:

> There was a high majestic fooling
> Day before yesterday in the yellow corn...

After high school Sandburg embarked upon a hobo period. He rode boxcars, waited tables, dug potatoes, washed windows, threshed wheat. In 1898, he volunteered for service in the Spanish-American War and was sent to Puerto Rico for eight months. Back in Galesburg, he used his discharge money for college tuition and enrolled at Lombard (now part of Knox College), where one of the crucial Lincoln-Douglas debates had been held in 1858. Before graduating, however, he took off and started wandering again, finally settling in Milwaukee, where he worked as a newspaper reporter. There he met a striking young woman, who had graduated with high honors in philosophy and was a sister of the famous American photographer Edward Steichen. Paula Steichen and Carl Sandburg married in 1908, and three years later, the young couple set out for Chicago.

Sandburg rejoiced in the energy and brutal strength he found in this industrial hub. The editor of the Chicago *Daily News* urged him to write about it, and he did so in prose that echoed the themes and style of Walt Whitman. He also received encouragement from another source. Harriet Monroe, founder of *Poetry* Magazine, welcomed Sandburg as a bold new voice. In 1914, Sandburg won his first award for a series of poems in *Poetry*, a series that included the now-famous "Chicago":

> Hog Butcher for the World,
> Tool Maker, Stacker of Wheat,
> Player with Railroads and the Nation's Freight Handler;
> Stormy, husky, brawling, City of the Big Shoulders.

He was a prolific poet (*too* prolific, according to some critics), and his *Collected Poems* included over eight hundred items. Many thought him best at brief lyric "spurts."

In 1923, Sandburg's career took a new turn. He signed a contract to write a Lincoln biography for boys. As he began to detect more and more similarities between Lincoln's life and his own, Sandburg's fascination with the Civil War President grew into an obsession. He described his work as "a book about a man whose mother could not sign her name, written by a man whose father could not sign his. Perhaps that could happen only in America." Gradually, the four-hundred-page book mushroomed into two volumes of over four thousand pages, the second of which—*The War Years*—won Sandburg a Pulitzer Prize.

In writing the biography, he said, he tried to search for "picture words such as the Indians and Chinese used."

> He [Lincoln] lived with trees, with the bush wet with shining raindrops, with the burning bush of autumn, with the lone wild ducks riding a north wind and crying down on a line north and south, the faces of open sky and weather.

For a change of pace from research and writing, Sandburg traveled cross-country on singing and speaking tours. His figure, bent over his guitar with his silver hair tumbling forward, became a familiar sight on the college lecture circuit. He sang folk songs in a lilting baritone, recited poems, and regaled his young audiences with stories about America in its frontier days. In this respect, Sandburg has often been compared to Robert Frost, but in truth the two men had little in common. Whereas Sandburg might bite off a whole chunk of humanity at one time:

> The people, yes.
> Out of what is their change
> from chaos to order
> and chaos again?

Frost always dealt in specifics. Where Frost worked hard at his craft, Sandburg was more spontaneous. Even their family lives differed strikingly. In contrast to Frost's troubled marriage, the partnership of Paula and Carl Sandburg was warm and loving. With three lively daughters, the house often rang with laughter. A friend of the family once said, "I have never been in a home before with an undivided feeling of harmony." In one of Carl Sandburg's many poems to his wife, he wrote,

> And the sheen of your hair is glory
> You are the sea with its mystic song.
> You are the stars and dawn and morning...

At Sandburg's death in 1967, President Lyndon Johnson declared, "The road has come to an end for Carl Sandburg, my friend and the good companion of millions whose own life journeys have been ennobled and enriched by his poetry... Carl Sandburg needs no epitaph. It is written for all time in the fields, the cities, the land he loved and the people he celebrated and inspired..."

THE DOUBLE LIFE OF WALLACE STEVENS
(1879–1955)

In 1951, when Wallace Stevens was given an honorary degree from Harvard, where he had attended college, the citation read,

> A man with a double life; versed in the intricacies of insurance, he portrays a stark America in word patterns of modern form.

His business associates at the Hartford Accident and Indemnity Company, hearing of the honor, were shocked. They had no idea that their tall, reserved colleague was one of the most highly regarded poets of the twentieth century.

This emphasis on privacy was typical of Stevens, and it is the chief reason that little is known of his childhood. From scraps of information, we can assume it was normal enough. He grew up in Reading, Pennsylvania, where his father was a lawyer. There were the usual schoolboy pranks—sneaking off to chew tobacco, for instance—but few hints of any large or lasting influences. One influence may have been his kindergarten, run by a French woman who possibly stimulated his lifelong love of the French language. Also the family spent summers at an old hotel in Ephrata, Pennsylvania, and Stevens's father would arrive on weekends carrying great baskets of pears, apples, grapes, and peaches, which the children devoured. Not surprisingly, Stevens's mature poems overflow with images of fruit:

> A pear should come to the table popped with juice,
> Ripened in warmth and served in warmth.

But the most persistent shapes were those of landscape, of mountains ("...The stars/Are shining on all bows of Neversink") and rivers ("The wood-doves are singing along the Perkiomen"). Later in life, these real images would be replaced in Stevens's mind by their re-creation in words:

> There it was, word for word,
> The poem that took the place of a mountain.
>
> He breathed its oxygen
> Even when the book lay turned in the dust of
> his table.
>
> It reminded him how he had needed
> A place to go to in his own direction...

Stevens began writing poetry as an undergraduate at Harvard (saying later, "Those poems give me the creeps"). When he left Harvard, he moved to New York and became a reporter for the New York *Tribune*. After a few months of sporadic assignments, he gave up the idea of journalism and, taking his father's advice, entered New York Law School. He was admitted to the bar in 1904. News of his admission arrived while he was enjoying a vacation in Reading.

It was on this vacation that he met a rather stiff but beautiful young lady named Elsie Kachel. Charmed by her shyness, Stevens began a courtship carried on mostly by mail. Five years later, he and Elsie Kachel were married.

It was to her he confided his most deeply held ambition:

> I have...been trying to get together a little collection
> of verses again... Keep this a great secret. There is
> something absurd about all this writing of verses; but
> the truth is, it elates and satisfies me to do it.

Meanwhile he was building his career as an insurance
lawyer. By 1914 he had become New York vice president
of the Equitable Surety Company of St. Louis. In that year,
he also sent a group of eight poems to Harriet Monroe,
who edited *Poetry* Magazine, the most influential poetry
publication in the country. No critic has fully explained
the astonishing leap from juvenile versifying—

> He sang, and in her heart, the sound
> Took form beyond the song's content.
> She saw divinely, and she felt
> With a visionary blandishment...

—to the absolute mastery of diction and subject matter in
poems such as "Sunday Morning":

> Why should she give her bounty to the dead?
> What is divinity if it can come
> Only in silent shadows and in dreams?
> Shall she not find in comforts of the sun,
> In pungent fruit and bright, green wings, or else
> In any balm or beauty of the earth,
> Things to be cherished like the thought of heaven?

Like other American writers of his time—attempting,
perhaps, to combat the clichés of public speech and public
life—Stevens felt called upon to reinvent the English
language. He made liberal use of obscure terms and odd
phrases that might have been muttered by some ancient,
elegant drunk in love with sheer sound ("The lacquered

loges huddled there/Mumbled zay-zay and a-zay, a-zay.")
But Stevens was at his best when a certain straightforward
attitude, also typically American, took over and he simply
told things as he saw them. He saw beautifully, with an
eccentric's taste for odd detail and a painter's eye for color:

> Coffee and oranges in a sunny chair,
> And the green freedom of a cockatoo
> Upon a rug...

Harriet Monroe, intrigued by this original voice, asked
for more poems and some biographical information.
Stevens sent the poems but was reluctant to speak about
himself. An acquaintance described Stevens as "a big,
slightly fat, awfully competent-looking man. You expect
him to roar, but when he speaks there emerges the gravest,
softest, most subtly modulated voice I've ever heard—a
voice on tiptoe at dawn..."

In 1916, a business associate brought Stevens into the
Hartford Accident and Indemnity Company. He and Elsie
were not sorry to exchange the urban chaos of New York
for a quieter city. Seven years after the move, Stevens's first
collection of poetry, *Harmonium*, was published, but it
unfortunately became lost in the hoopla surrounding T. S.
Eliot's *The Waste Land*, which appeared in 1922. After
what he considered the failure of *Harmonium*, Stevens
stopped writing for almost a decade. Instead, he immersed
himself in the insurance business. He sometimes
complained about the time consumed by his work:

> One never gets anywhere in writing or thinking or
> observing unless one can do so for long stretches...
> Often when I have a real fury for indulgence, I must
> stint myself. Of course, we must all do the same thing...
> If farmers had summers ten years long, what tomatoes
> they could grow, and if sailors had universal seas what
> voyages they could take.

But the bohemian artistic life never appealed to Stevens. He enjoyed fine cigars, paintings, well-tailored suits, and all the other accessories that made him somewhat of a dandy. "Money is a kind of poetry," he was fond of saying, as if defending his affluence.

Yet no one, with the possible exception of the German poet Rainer Maria Rilke, had written and talked about poetry as Stevens did. To him it was a sanction, a permission that validated the fact of existing. To create a poem was to create oneself. "To practice an art," he once wrote, "to need it and to love it, is the quickest way of learning that all happiness lies in one's self, as Omar Khayyám [a Persian poet and author of *The Rubáiyát*] says it does."

A large part of Stevens's life was spent in almost complete solitude. He would work at his insurance office all day, and then come home and read, or write, or listen to music. In his own way, he was as much of an exile as Ezra Pound or T. S. Eliot, except that his exile was mental rather than geographic. Although foreign places fascinated him, his wife was a terrible traveler and was constantly carsick or seasick whenever she went anywhere. So Stevens set up imaginary trips through acquaintances who journeyed and lived abroad and were willing to send him postcards, pictures, books, teas, and figurines—offerings that sparked his imagination. "If I should ever go to Paris," he once said, "the first person I should meet there would probably be myself. I have been there so often."

Stevens published six more books of poetry and a book of essays. But honors came to him only in the last five years of his life. He won the Bollingen Prize for Poetry in 1950 and a National Book Award in 1951. Following the publication of his *Collected Poems* in 1954, Stevens received another National Book Award, then a Pulitzer Prize, in 1955. To his surprise, his insurance colleagues, after the first shock had worn off, were delighted to have a poet in their midst. At last his double life was merging into one. He was content to be known as a poet *and* a businessman, and his perception had finally reached that stage of fluency when what is real and what is imagined become the same. According to one of his last poems, "It was like/A new knowledge of reality."

William Carlos William

THE STRUGGLE OF WILLIAM CARLOS WILLIAMS TO BE AMERICAN (1883–1963)

For over forty years of his life, William Carlos Williams was a practicing physician. In between patients he jotted down descriptions—quick, concise images of the life around him—on prescription pads. Of course his patients had no inkling that the kindly doctor holding a stethoscope to their chests was also a poet—and, indeed, a poet who in his spare time was in the process of changing the course of American poetry.

Dr. Williams had strong feelings about America, its past and future. He believed that poetry should affirm the democratic principles that had somehow become misplaced in America's obsession with money. He also believed that poetry should be "local" and concrete. It should focus on everyday objects and common people.

> ..It should
>
> be a song—made of
> particulars, wasps,
> a gentian—something
> immediate, open
>
> > scissors, a lady's
> > eyes...

Nowadays these beliefs seem quite commonplace. In

1910, however, when the most serious young American writers were fleeing to Europe in hopes of finding something more exotic than their native land could offer, they were unusual. By remaining behind in Rutherford, New Jersey, attending the sick, observing and recording what he saw and felt in thin, terse lines, Williams placed himself in direct opposition to the exiles.

The reason for Williams' stubborn patriotism probably stemmed from the foreign origins of both his parents, who had settled in Rutherford in the late nineteenth century. His mother had been born in Puerto Rico (of French, Dutch, Spanish, and Jewish ancestry), and his father was English. Wishing to become model immigrants, they expected their son to be perfect, too, in both behavior and speech, an almost impossible goal for an adolescent approaching college age. By the time he reached the University of Pennsylvania, where he decided to study medicine, the emotional straitjacket was becoming a torment. Then he discovered the expansive poetry of Walt Whitman.

In Whitman, Williams saw the kind of freedom of impulse that he himself longed to possess. Gradually, he began to make his first stabs at writing. His mentor at the university was a fellow poetry enthusiast named Ezra Pound (see page 51). Pound supported Williams in his instinctive desire to reject "genteel" rhymes and find a more direct expression of emotions and surroundings. Just when Williams was beginning to achieve his first success, however, Pound departed for Europe.

Finishing medical school, Williams returned to Rutherford, opened an office, married a local woman, Florence Herman, and settled down to an outwardly conventional life: playing with his two small sons, answering emergency calls, chatting with neighbors. Yet, inside his head, images were boiling. Letters between him and Pound crossed the Atlantic, with Williams sending his

latest efforts for Pound's criticism.

Gradually, the name of another American poet living abroad began to crop up in Pound's letters. He reported that this poet, T. S. Eliot, was creating (with Pound's help) a "masterpiece." When the masterpiece, *The Waste Land*, appeared in print in 1922, Williams was stunned. Philosophic where his own poetry was concrete, European in flavor where his own was American, *The Waste Land* seemed the exact opposite of what he had been trying to do. As Eliot's popularity spread, Williams grumbled, "My contemporaries flock to him [Eliot], away from what I want." But his disappointment strengthened his determination to fight for the future of American poetry.

For three decades, virtually cut off from any meaningful audience, he published poem after poem in little magazines. Then, slowly, younger poets such as Allen Ginsberg, Denise Levertov, and Robert Creeley, recognizing the merit of Williams' work, gathered around him. Buoyed by their admiration, Williams embarked on a long epic poem, *Paterson* (named for the town of Paterson, New Jersey). With *Paterson*, the honors that had earlier been denied Williams began to pour in. He won the National Book Award for poetry in 1950, the Bollingen Prize in 1952, the Academy of American Poets fellowship in 1956 and, finally, in the year of his death, the Pulitzer Prize. The last part of *Paterson*, written after Williams had retired from medical practice, proclaimed the power of the imagination over the dwindling powers of the body in old age.

EZRA POUND, LITERARY IMPRESARIO
(1885–1972)

Although Ezra Pound grew up in a Philadelphia suburb, he had someone to give him a broader perspective: his "Aunt Frank." Aunt Frank ran a boarding house in New York where Ezra often spent weekends. When he was thirteen, she took him and his mother abroad on a trip that changed his life. They toured the cathedral towns of France and the art palaces of northern Italy, including Florence and Venice.

At fifteen, he entered the University of Pennsylvania, where upperclassmen, put off by his brash, arrogant manner as well as his loud socks, threw him into a lily pond full of cold water. Undaunted, the new freshman appeared the next day wearing socks even louder than before. This incident was one of the early signs of Pound's willingness to buck authority. The tendency would one day prove disastrous.

In spite of meeting two other students who became lasting friends—the poets Hilda Doolittle (or "H.D.") and William Carlos Williams—Pound disliked the university's restrictions and soon switched to Hamilton College, which was more suited to his temperament. Encouraged by professors who recognized the young student's budding genius, he was allowed to pursue his own course of studies, which included Anglo-Saxon and Old French (useful for translating the medieval troubadour poets).

> If all the grief and woe and bitterness,
> All dolour, ill and every evil chance
> That ever came upon this grieving world
> Were set together they would seem but light
> Against the death of the young English King.
>
> *(from the Provençal of Bertran de Born, on*
> *the death of Prince Henry Plantagenet)*

But the most profound literary influence during this period, and perhaps for the rest of his life, was Dante's *Divine Comedy*, which Pound praised for its precision of language and detail. He wrote home, "...find me a phenomenon of any importance in the lives of men and nations that you cannot measure with the rod of Dante's allegory." *The Divine Comedy* would form the basis for his own masterpiece, the *Cantos*.

After graduating from Hamilton, Pound took a job as English instructor at Wabash College in Crawfordsville, Indiana. Although it billed itself as "the Athens of the Midwest" and contained several theaters, Crawfordsville, in fact, was a small provincial outpost. But Pound quickly identified a few of the more interesting students and faculty and invited them to weekly gatherings in his rooms. An infrequent guest at these events provided a sarcastic description:

> After the preliminary formalities, Pound seated himself on a chair, while his disciples and satellites disposed themselves gracefully, but somewhat uncomfortably, cross-legged on the floor, at the foot of the master. The leader then began a spirited but disconnected discourse on many topics, leaping from subject to subject with the agility of a mountain goat.

During the second semester, Pound was dismissed for

"behavior unbecoming a professor." The behavior, according to Pound himself, was based on an innocent gesture: rescuing a stranded actress by giving her a place to stay for the night. But the dismissal strengthened his determination to go abroad. His father, Homer, agreed to give his son enough money for cheap boat passage if Ezra could offer proof that his poetry held promise. Ezra boldly sent a manuscript to the poetry editor of a famous magazine, disclosing his dilemma. The editor invited the young poet to New York, and later recounted the interview—and Ezra's costume:

> I should say that his jacket, trousers and vest had each a brave color, with a main effect of purple and yellow, that one shoe was tan, the other blue, and that on a shiny straw hat the ribbon was white with red polka dots...

But in spite of Pound's flamboyance, the editor wrote his father a glowing report. Several weeks later, Ezra Pound sailed for Europe. He went first to Venice, the city of his dreams, but could not find enough work to make a living. On leaving, he composed this farewell,

> Ne'er felt I parting from a woman loved
> As feel I now my going forth from thee...

Traveling to England, Pound managed to make the acquaintance of William Butler Yeats—the leading English-speaking poet—and secure a position as Yeats's secretary. (He later married the daughter of the woman who had introduced them.) Now began a period of furious activity. He made it his business to meet the most important editors, writers, and critics in London; then he proceeded to persuade, cajole, and bully them into doing what he wanted. Thinking of himself as a literary impresario, or talent manager, he evoked the word's original meaning: someone—in the days of medieval chivalry—who undertook an important mission. Through Yeats, Pound met James Joyce and helped him get his novel *Ulysses* published. He did the same with T.S. Eliot's first poems. He was largely responsible for Robert Frost's gaining recognition in America.

By 1920, England was beginning to lose some of its original appeal and he and his wife moved to Paris, where he struck up a friendship with Ernest Hemingway. During this period, he also served as midwife for the birth of Eliot's *The Waste Land*. In gratitude, Eliot dedicated the poem to Pound with the Italian inscription *il miglior fabbro*, meaning "the better craftsman."

Eager to find a quiet place to work on the *Cantos*, the Pounds next settled in northern Italy. The *Cantos*, on which Pound worked for many years, was to be an epic dialogue with the vast panorama of history. For a while, the setting brought a calmness that was reflected in the poetry:

Autumn moon; hills rise about lakes
against sunset
Evening is like a curtain of cloud
a blur above ripples; and through it
sharp long spikes of the cinnamon,
a cold tune amid reeds.
Behind hill the monk's bell
borne on the wind.
Sail passed here in April; may return in October
Boat fades in silver; slowly...

(*from* Canto XLIX)

But in the 1930s, Pound began to rant again, and this time a peevishness crept into his tone. Declaring the Italian dictator Benito Mussolini "a genius," he supported the Fascist government and publicly railed against the capitalistic "money-mad" policies of the United States. Some began to fear for Pound's sanity. His daughter Mary wrote, "He was...losing grip on what most specifically he should have been able to control, his own *words*."

At the war's end, in 1945, he was taken into custody as an American traitor. Then began the ticklish business of deciding what to do with him. The official solution was to place him in a mental institution—St. Elizabeth's Hospital in Washington, D.C. Calling it a "hell-hole," Pound wrote,

> Dementia
> mental torture...
> a world lost...
> coherent areas
>   constantly
>   invaded
>   aiuto ("Help!")

Friends like Eliot, Hemingway, and even Frost *did* try to help, but it took twelve years to secure his release. In 1958, Pound was finally allowed to return to Italy. There, younger poets, such as Allen Ginsberg, went to pay him homage. Now distrusting words, Pound, the old impresario, received many of these tributes in silence.

T. S. ELIOT: AMERICAN OR ENGLISH?
(1888–1965)

When T. S. Eliot first stepped onto British soil in 1910, he had no notion that the visit would last a lifetime. Having just graduated from Harvard University, he had traveled abroad to soak up as much foreign culture as his puritanical background would allow. (The Eliot family had migrated to St. Louis, Missouri, from New England, where they were strong Unitarians.)

Eliot returned to Harvard briefly, but by late 1914 he was back across the Atlantic—at Oxford University to work on his doctoral degree in philosophy. He also began writing poetry and criticism.

During this period, three momentous events took place. The first was an encounter with another American poet, Ezra Pound, who had arrived abroad several years earlier. After Eliot showed Pound some of his poetry, Pound immediately took on the role of mentor and adviser. It was Pound who paved the way for Eliot's first published book of poems, *Prufrock and Other Observations*, in 1917. The title poem, "The Love Song of J. Alfred Prufrock," anticipates some of the same themes and techniques that will recur in Eliot's longer work:

- a concern with time;
- images that symbolize states of mind;

- repetition;
- an intuition that modern poetry should reflect the complexities of experience;
- an acquired British flavor that has little to do with the cadence and speech of his native country.

Here is a small excerpt from "Prufrock." Notice how Eliot uses an animal image (possibly a cat, which was his favorite pet) to depict the fog:

> The yellow fog that rubs its back upon the window-
>   panes,
> The yellow smoke that rubs its muzzle on the window-
>   panes,
> Licked its tongue into the corners of the evening,
> Lingered upon the pools that stand in drains,
> Let fall upon its back the soot that falls from chimneys,
> Slipped by the terrace, made a sudden leap,
> And seeing that it was a soft October night,
> Curled once about the house, and fell asleep.

The second momentous event was the outbreak of World War I in 1914. At this point, one might have expected Eliot to return to America, but he didn't. As one of his friends remarked, by then Eliot was "out-Englishing the English." A British accent had replaced his youthful midwestern drawl, and he habitually wore a bowler hat and carried a tightly rolled umbrella, the props of a British bank clerk.

Third, the same month that "Prufrock" appeared in print, Eliot eloped with a high-strung young woman he had met at an Oxford party. When Eliot sailed to America (alone) to break the news to his family, they were shocked. His father, feeling rejected, refused to have anything more to do with him.

Back in England, Eliot settled down to a life of teaching school during the day and writing in the evening. But his happiness was short-lived. His wife proved to be mentally

unstable and eventually had to be institutionalized. As a result of the strain, Eliot himself suffered a nervous breakdown. He went to a seaside resort near London for treatment, then to Lausanne in Switzerland. On the way, he stopped off in Paris to show Ezra Pound the first draft of an ambitious and lengthy poem that was a collage of images. Pound quickly recognized the poem's originality and, after making some cuts and suggestions, proceeded to advertise its uniqueness to all his literary friends. With Pound's approval, Eliot titled the poem *The Waste Land*.

When the poem was first published, in 1922, readers were puzzled by its difficulties. It seemed to raise more questions than it answered. Yet a devastating war had made people wary of easy solutions, and soon it became the most widely discussed and frequently analyzed poem in England, and later in America. Here is the beginning of *The Waste Land*.

> April is the cruellest month, breeding
> Lilacs out of the dead land, mixing
> Memory and desire, stirring
> Dull roots with spring rain...

When Eliot joined the Church of England and became a naturalized British citizen in 1927, his transferral of allegiance from one country to another was almost complete. But no one's past can ever be completely erased, and the third part of *Four Quartets* (which Eliot considered his finest work) strongly echoes the Missouri and Massachusetts background of his youth.

> ...I think that the river
> Is a strong brown god—sullen, untamed and
> intractable...

Although Eliot won the esteemed Nobel Prize for Literature in 1948, he confessed to friends that such an honor seemed empty without someone to share it. Then, in the last decade of his life, he fell in love with his secretary in the publishing firm of Faber & Faber (where he worked as an editorial director) and married her. From all evidence, this second marriage brought him the warmth and devotion that had been missing from his first.

Toward the end of his life, Eliot expressed wishes for his ashes to be placed in the cemetery of East Coker in Somerset, the home of the Eliots before they had sailed to the New World. Perhaps it was his way of completing a cycle. Perhaps it was a further sign of loyalty to his adopted country. Yet in truth, T. S. Eliot belongs to *two* cultures—American and English—one buried beneath the other but often emerging in an unexpected insight or depth of feeling.

Langston Hughes

LANGSTON HUGHES AND THE BLACK EXPERIENCE (1902–1967)

Langston Hughes was fond in later life of relating an ironic story about how he became a poet. It happened when he was in the seventh grade in Lincoln, Illinois, where he lived for a year. "They [the classmates] had elected all the class officers, but class poet. There were two Negro children in the class, myself and a girl. In America most white people think, of course, that *all* Negroes can sing and dance, and have a sense of rhythm. So my classmates, knowing that a poem had to have rhythm, elected me unanimously, thinking, no doubt, that I had some, being a Negro." One of his duties as class poet was to write and recite a poem at elementary school graduation, a task that, with some assistance from his mother, he carried out handsomely. The applause was so heartening that he decided, then and there, to be a poet.

At that point Hughes needed all the applause he could get. His father had left home when Hughes was an infant, and he and his mother had gone to live with his grandmother in Lawrence, Kansas. Though his mother would continue to flit in and out of his life, his grandmother raised him. It was she who instilled in him a sense of pride about his forebears, one of whom led the rescue of fugitive slaves before the Civil War.

When he was seven, Hughes's aged grandmother grew increasingly silent and distant, and he had to fall back on other resources. The first was books. "Then it was that books began to happen to me, and I began to believe in nothing but books and the wonderful world in books— where if people suffered, they suffered in beautiful language, not in monosyllables, as we did in Kansas." The second resource was church and the ecstatic religious feelings that emerged there.

> Glory! Hallelujah!
> The dawn's a-comin'!
> Glory! Hallelujah!
> The dawn's a-comin'!

But church was not all shouting and swaying. The church Hughes attended often held debates and musicales, which sometimes featured black students from the nearby University of Kansas. These occasions gave Hughes a sense of the potential of black people that was often buried under the poverty and neglect he saw around him.

The most significant event, however—at least in terms of his poetry—took place in a barber shop run by an uncle. It was here he first heard the blues.

> I got de weary blues
> And I can't be satisfied.
> Got de weary blues
> And can't be satisfied.

Blues music had originated in the South in response to black slavery. It took the form of "field hollers"—musical dialogues between groups of field hands—and work songs. Both of these had their roots in West Africa, where melodies were sung in leader-chorus, call-and-response style. The blues are usually an expression of despair—sometimes about love, more often about everyday life. But an upbeat

feeling can emerge from the blues, as if the act of expressing a painful feeling purges or transforms it.

Although the blues are improvisational, there is a basic twelve-bar structure. The first line might go: "When a woman gets the blues/she wrings her hands and cries." This is repeated with an additional word or phrase: "*I said*, when a woman gets the blues, she wrings her hands and cries." This repetition is for emphasis and to give the singer time to improvise the contrasting response, usually with a rhyme: "But when a man gets the blues, he grabs a train and rides."

Hughes became the first poet to treat the blues as a legitimate style for poetry. His genius lay in realizing the effectiveness of its repetitions to convey suffering and despondency. Not only did he employ the basic blues pattern, but, like his counterparts in music, he also improvised numerous variations on it.

> Where is that sugar, Hammond,
> I sent you this morning to buy?
> I say, where is that sugar
> I sent you this morning to buy?
> Coffee without sugar
> Makes a good woman cry...

After graduating from high school in 1920, Hughes yearned for a reconciliation with his father and took a train to Mexico, where his father was living. Although the meeting was disappointing, the trip itself provided Hughes with the inspiration for one of his most notable poems. It came to him, he said, just as the train was crossing the Mississippi River at sunset.

> I've known rivers:
> I've known rivers ancient as the world and older
>   than the flow of human blood in human veins.
> My soul has grown deep like the rivers...

The poem was included in his first book of poetry, *The Weary Blues*, published in 1926.

Over a forty-year span, Hughes wrote sixteen volumes of poems, two novels, three collections of short stories, twenty dramatic pieces, eight children's books, two volumes of autobiography, and twelve radio and television scripts. He was the first black writer to support himself solely by his writing. During the 1930s, '40s, and '50s, he was the most influential of the black poets, and many young people sought him out for advice. During the 1960s, however, some militant blacks belittled his achievement. In spite of this, he continued writing until his death in 1967. Only recently have critics begun to reassess the work of Langston Hughes, and to understand the debt owed him for his poetic originality and for focusing attention on the suffering, endurance, and beauty of his people.

Pablo Neruda

PABLO NERUDA: GIFTS UNDER THE FENCE
(1904–1973)

In his *Memoirs*, the Chilean poet Pablo Neruda writes,

> I also recall that one day, while hunting behind my
> house for the tiny objects...of my world, I discovered
> a hole in one of the fence boards. I looked through the
> opening and saw a patch of land just like ours, untended
> and wild. I drew back a few steps, because I had a
> vague feeling that something was about to happen.
> Suddenly a hand came through. It was the small hand
> of a boy my own age. When I moved closer, the hand
> was gone and in its place was a little white sheep.
>
> It was a sheep made of wool that had faded. The
> wheels on which it had glided were gone. I had never
> seen such a lovely sheep. I went into my house and
> came back with a gift, which I left in the same place:
> a pine cone, partly open, fragrant and resinous, and
> very precious to me.
>
> I never saw the boy's hand again. I have never again
> seen a little sheep like that one...

Although Neruda doesn't say so directly, he suggests
that writing poetry is somewhat like putting a gift under
the fence for an unknown person.

Pablo Neruda started "putting gifts under fences" at
fifteen, when he sent poems off to the literary magazine

Selva Austral. Instead of signing his real name, Ricardo Eliecer Neftalí y Basoalto, he adopted the surname of a popular nineteenth-century Czech writer, Jan Neruda, as his pseudonym.

An indifferent student, Neruda won recognition at college by entering a poetry competition and winning. His first published collection, *Crepusculario (Twilight)*, appeared in 1923. This book of poems reflected his interest in symbolism—the use of objects, persons, places, or events that signify something over and above their literal meaning. Later volumes would reveal Neruda's ties with surrealism—a twentieth-century movement in the arts that tried to express inner realities by rejecting logical sequences of time and space.

During the 1960s, Neruda's poems began to be translated into English. Many of these took the form of odes, or poems of praise. Others were elegiac—that is, concerned with death or dying.

> because grief taught us to be,
> because the hands' work is a destiny
> and life shapes itself to their scars.

The surrealistic quality of these poems—which emphasized the imaginative over the literal—profoundly affected younger writers:

> we must pound out
> the mud like a batter
> till it sings;
> all must be soiled with our tears,
> washed with our blood,...
> till a river leaps forth,
> the whole of a river
> in the span of a tea-cup;
> so goes the song:
> that is the word
> for a river.

Many writers, especially Latin Americans, followed Neruda's cue in actively participating in life, rather than remaining at its edge as an onlooker. Pablo Neruda was never simply a spectator. Besides being a poet, he was a diplomat and, in his younger years, a revolutionary who fought to help the cause of poor people in his native Chile. He wrote over forty books of poetry that have been translated into numerous languages. Two years before he died in 1973, he won the Nobel Prize for Literature. Neruda has been called one of the greatest poets of the Spanish world, and one of the major poets of the twentieth century.

Theodore Roethke

THEODORE ROETHKE: THE LOST SON
(1908–1963)

Sigmund Freud, the "father of psychoanalysis," once remarked that the death of a father is the most significant event in a man's life. Although this is a vast generalization, it was certainly true of Theodore Roethke. In Roethke's second year of high school, his father died of cancer. Outwardly, young Roethke—or "Ted" as he was called—appeared unmoved. But the image of his parent and their early association would haunt him the rest of his life.

Roethke was born in Saginaw, Michigan, where his grandfather, a German immigrant, had started a market garden. The family business was continued by his father, Otto, and his uncle, Karl. Roethke grew up in a world of plants, dirt, fertilizers, greenhouses, bulbs, molds.

> Where were the greenhouses going,
> Lunging into the lashing
> Wind driving water
> So far down the river
> All the faucets stopped?

Much of his childhood was spent in bed, recovering from either pneumonia or bronchitis. Perhaps it was this sickly disposition that fed the intense self-dramatization that characterized a good part of Roethke's adult life. At the

University of Michigan, for instance, he bought himself a raccoon coat in which he lumbered around campus. Since the purchase coincided with his growing ambition to be a poet, it may have been an effort to develop a tough-guy image and stave off ridicule.

After graduate school, Roethke took a teaching position at Lafayette, a small college in Pennsylvania. He liked teaching and proved to be popular with students. During this period he started writing his first serious poems.

It was at his next post, Michigan State College, that he suffered a mental breakdown and had to be hospitalized. It started with a walk in the woods, where Roethke experienced some sort of mystical vision that gradually turned into delirium. The trauma left him shaken and terrified. He returned to Saginaw and slowly began to recover; then, in the fall of 1937, he accepted a job at Pennsylvania State University. Two years later his first book of poems, *The Open House*, was published. Although the book received good notices, Roethke still had not found his poetic voice; his genuine feelings were cramped by the use of formal, strict meters. This would soon change.

Stanley Kunitz, a poet and friend, had read some of Roethke's recent poems about his father and advised him to continue mining this personal vein. The result was *The Lost Son*, which critics praised for its originality of content: man's relationship with his evolutionary past. In vivid language, Roethke captured the oneness of nature that remains in the brain in spite of our struggle to become "civilized."

> And what a congress of stinks!
> Roots ripe as old bait,
> Pulpy stems, rank, silo-rich,
> Leaf-mold, manure, lime, piled against slippery planks.
> Nothing would give up life:
> Even the dirt kept breathing a small breath.

Now began the happiest period in Roethke's life. Not only was he recognized as a major American poet, but he also took a teaching position at the University of Washington in Seattle, where he was able to transfer his excitement about poetry and the writing process to such talented students as James Wright and David Waggoner. He also married and made several trips abroad. In 1954, he won the Pulitzer Prize.

In spite of two more nervous breakdowns, Roethke continued writing to the end of his life. His last book, *The Far Field*, was published after his death. The final sequence ends with these lines:

> Now I adore my life
> With the Bird, the abiding Leaf,
> With the Fish, the questing Snail,
> And the Eye altering all;
> And I dance with William Blake
> For love, for Love's sake;
>
> And everything comes to One,
> As we dance on, dance on, dance on.

Louis Simpson (signature)

LOUIS SIMPSON: A NEW COLUMBUS (1923–)

The poet/critic Donald Hall has called Louis Simpson "the Columbus of an inward continent." Not only does Simpson explore this inward continent, but he also urges the rest of us to pay more attention to its inventions.

> I must be patient with shapes
> Of automobile fenders and ketchup bottles.
> These things are the beginning
>
> Of things not visible to the naked eye.
> It was so in the time of Tobit—
> The dish glowed when the angel held it.

Simpson grew up on a mountain in a remote part of Jamaica. When his parents divorced, his mother moved to the United States, and her son came with her. He studied at Columbia University and went into the U.S. Army in 1943. After World War II ended two years later, he held a number of jobs—including that of editor at a publishing house—before settling down to writing and teaching. He has taught at the University of California at Berkeley and at the State University of New York at Stony Brook, Long Island.

Louis Simpson's early poems display technical skill but lack a distinctive voice. A turning point came with his

fourth collection, *At the End of the Open Road*. By this time he had found his theme: the death of the American dream of ever-expanding progress and success. In the nineteenth century, Walt Whitman had celebrated the vast potential of America. Simpson writes:

> Whitman was wrong about the People,
> But right about himself. The land is within.
> At the end of the open road we come to ourselves.

Not only is the dream dead, but something is wrong with "the inner part" of the country itself, its values and ideals.

> Priests, examining the entrails of birds,
> Found the heart misplaced, and seeds
> As black as death, emitting a strange odor.

In subsequent books, Simpson has continued to explore the same theme in different ways. How does the poet live in a country where "the thought of the mind" has such little value, he asks. Not by escaping from it, the answer comes, but by constant vigilance over both the "kingdom within" and the "kingdom without":

> Your loves are a line of birch trees.
> When the wind flattens the grass, it
> shines, and a butterfly
> Writes dark lines on the air.

> These are your sacred objects,
> the wings and gazing eyes
> of the life you really have.

ROBERT BLY: TWO KINDS OF CONSCIOUSNESS (1926–)

Robert Bly has been a leading force in American poetry since the 1950s. Bly dislikes the "confessional" style of poets such as Robert Lowell and Sylvia Plath, who recorded in verse their most intense inner conflicts. Instead, Bly celebrates the human capacity to identify with an outside world, particularly the world of nature.

Bly grew up outside Madison, Minnesota. After finishing his university studies, he married and settled down on a farm near his old family home. In 1958, he started a magazine called *The Fifties* (which subsequently became *The Sixties* and *The Seventies*), in which the works of many foreign poets, including Pablo Neruda, were introduced. In their work, Bly discovered a "poetry which is not dying but growing, poetry which has found a way to include not only more of the mood of modern life than any before, but also more of the joy of the unconscious."

Bly says of his first collection, *Silence in the Snowy Fields*, "Nearly all the poems were written at dusk, and the passages from day to night, and that's possibly a time when the unconscious appears." He tried to capture the sudden bursts of discovery that might be found in such appearances.

> If I reached my hands down, near the earth
> I could take handfuls of darkness!

In the late 1960s, during the Vietnam War, Bly took a strong anti-war position. As a result, his poetry grew increasingly strident and less visionary.

> We will have
> To go far away
> To atone
> For the sufferings of the stringy-chested
> And the small rice-fed ones, quivering
> In the helicopters like wild animals...

In his later books, however—notably *This Tree Will Be Here for a Thousand Years*—he returns to the idea of a poetry that goes beyond the self, even the political self. Describing the poems, Bly says they "contain an instant, sometimes twenty seconds long, sometimes longer, when I was aware of two separate energies." Bly calls these energies the "outer consciousness" and the "inner consciousness." The outer consciousness is observation, whereas the inner consciousness is the imagination's response to observation. In some poems, these are separate; in others, they merge to create startling images that go a step beyond those in *Silence in the Snowy Fields*:

> Sometimes when you put your hand into a hollow tree
> you touch the dark places between stars.

Several of the images hint at the existence of a third consciousness, one more ancient and mysterious than the other two:

> The horse's hoof kicks up a seashell, and the farmer
> finds an Indian stone with a hole all the way through.

Allen Ginsberg

ALLEN GINSBERG AND THE BEAT POETS
(1926–)

On a summer evening in 1955, a young graduate of
Columbia University stood up in a San Francisco art gallery
and began reading a poem called "Howl," enthralling an
audience made up mostly of other artists. Allen Ginsberg's
closest friends—Jack Kerouac, Kenneth Rexroth, Neal
Cassady, and Lawrence Ferlinghetti—were scattered
throughout the crowd to lend moral support. Whenever
Ginsberg came to the end of a long line, Kerouac would
yell, "Go, go, go!"

"It was an ideal evening," Ginsberg recalled later, "and
I felt so pleased with the sense of 'at last a community.'
Jack said, 'Ginsberg, this poem "Howl" will make you
famous in San Francisco.' But Rexroth said, 'No, this poem
will make you famous from bridge to bridge,' which
sounded like an exaggeration, but I guess it's true."
Ginsberg's fame, indeed, later spread from San Francisco's
Golden Gate to New York's Brooklyn Bridge.

Here was a startling new kind of poetry. "Howl" was
not the bland verse of academic poets. It was raucous and
frankly political, written to be read aloud to crowds. It
was an enraged, sometimes outrageous, assault on the
mindless consumerism and conformity of a society heavily
influenced by advertising. It was also a plea that this society

turn to more human and humane values. The poem begins: "I saw the best minds of my generation destroyed by madness... " Then, in a relentless chant, it attacks Moloch, a tyrannical pagan deity appeased only by human sacrifice:

> What sphinx of cement and aluminum bashed open
>   their skulls and ate up their brains and imagination?
> Moloch! Solitude! Filth! Ugliness! Ashcans and
>   unobtainable dollars! Children screaming under the
>   stairways! Boys sobbing in armies! Old men weeping
>   in the parks!...

Many critics dismissed Ginsberg's words as "tiresome rhetoric," but that did not prevent the emergence of a new literary movement—poems, novels, and films of the "Beat Generation"—with its message of personal freedom and communal hope.

But Ginsberg's poetry is not all angry. In a comically surreal poem written shortly after "Howl," he invokes Walt Whitman to accompany him as he looks for meaning in "A Supermarket in California."

> What thoughts I have of you tonight, Walt Whitman,
>   for I walked down the sidestreets under the trees with
>   a headache self-conscious looking at the full moon.

> In my hungry fatigue, and shopping for images, I went
>   into the neon supermarket, dreaming of your
>   enumerations!

> What peaches and what penumbras! Whole families
>   shopping at night! Aisles full of husbands! Wives in
>   the avocados, babies in the tomatoes!—and you,
>   Garcia Lorca, what were you doing by the
>   watermelons?

Ginsberg and other Beat writers, such as Gregory Corso, Peter Orlovsky, and Jack Kerouac, believed that true riches were to be found in spiritual and artistic illumination. This

illumination might come from writing or painting, from ordinary moments with friends, or in solitary meditation. Such an experience happened to Ginsberg while reading "Ah, Sun-Flower" in William Blake's *Songs of Experience*. Suddenly the poem began to "speak aloud" in what he believed to be Blake's voice. "I felt everything vibrating in one harmony," Ginsberg said, "all past efforts and desires, all present realizations.... Everything was vibrating toward this one instant of consciousness." When he related the experience to friends, many of them thought he was crazy. "Had I been transported to a street-corner potato-curry shop in Benares [India] and begun acting that way," he muses, "I would have been seen as in some special, holy sort of state, and sent on my way... to sit and meditate." Ginsberg later called this Blakean vision a central point in his life, one that deeply affected his poetry.

Denouncing the rat race and "a buttoned-down life," the Beats were continually on the move. (Jack Kerouac's most famous work was aptly titled *On the Road*.) In 1961, Ginsberg and Orlovsky left on a global adventure that took them to India, Cambodia, Japan, and Czechoslovakia, where Ginsberg was crowned King of May and pulled through the streets in a rose-covered chariot. Returning to America in 1965, Ginsberg played the role of self-styled prophet to students disenchanted with the Vietnam War and the politics that had provoked it. He traveled to colleges and universities around the country reading his poems and advising his young audiences on everything from how to chant a Hindu or Buddhist mantra to how to avoid the draft. Many came to Ginsberg's readings out of curiosity, expecting to see a freak, but left disarmed by his honesty and gentleness.

Ginsberg's apocalyptic vision flows out of the moment, in what he calls "the holiness of the impulse." Sometimes his visions transcend these impulses, sometimes not. But there is little doubt of his place in history as the leading light of the Beats—that motley, talented group whose name, he claims, stands for "beatific."

JOHN ASHBERY: THE POET AS
EXPERIMENTALIST (1927–)

John Ashbery grew up on a farm near Rochester, New York. An only child, he has described his childhood as being "isolated" and lonely. After graduate school, he went to Paris, where he worked as art critic for the European edition of the New York *Herald Tribune*. He also began publishing poetry, much of which reflected his interest in the current art scene and in the work of the French surrealists. Surrealism was a movement that extolled imagination over rationalism. In order to keep the imagination alive and vibrant, the surrealists incorporated random encounters and spontaneous writing into their work.

Ashbery's first book, *Some Trees*, won the Yale Series of Younger Poets Award in 1956. In this early work, the influence of Wallace Stevens is evident, especially in poems that seem to chart the interior of the imagination:

> …you and I
> Are suddenly what the trees try
> To tell us we are…

Other poems offered more definite subject mattter:

> Sitting between the sea and the buildings
> He enjoyed painting the sea's portrait.

But just as children imagine a prayer
Is merely silence, he expected his subject
To rush up the sand, and, seizing a brush,
Plaster its own portrait on the canvas...

In his later books, Ashbery dropped all pretense of definite subject, and he continued to experiment. Sometimes his experiments worked, sometimes not. He explained in an interview,

> I think when there is a poem—take a poem of the past, for instance—where the meaning is perfectly clear, the subject matter is common knowledge and it's the other things that get included into the poem that raise it to the level of poetry and which are therefore the vital elements in the poem...this I think is the area that I write in to the exclusion of a formal theme or topic.

Another of Ashbery's sustaining beliefs concerns the balance between randomness and meaningfulness. He feels that meaningfulness exists in proportion to the strength of randomness (or chance occurrences). But to make randomness part of the work requires enormous self-confidence and a willingness to keep one's options open. It also requires a mind that can edit itself with some degree of insight.

This leaving-out business. On it hinges the very
importance of what's novel
Or autocratic, or dense or silly.

At the same time, he is

　　　 . . . not ready
To line phrases with the costly stuff of
explanation...

During the 1960s, Ashbery returned to New York and became executive editor of *Art News*. By the time he left

the magazine seven years later for a teaching position, he had published over a dozen books of poetry. Possibly his best-known book—the one that captured three major prizes, including a Pulitzer—is *Self-Portrait in a Convex Mirror*. In the central poem, Ashbery reflects on a self-portrait by the Italian painter Parmigianino (1503–1540). By distorting the perspective, the painter seems to convey certain truths about himself and his setting. Ashbery's poem also distorts. It magnifies peripheral ideas—ideas that lie at the edge of the conscious mind.

> The soul establishes itself.
> But how far can it swim out through the eyes
> And still return safely to its nest?

Many of Ashbery's poems are difficult. (He himself once called them "fables that time invents to explain its passing.") Yet there is no denying that he is at the forefront of modern poetry. In fact, the thrust of his poems seems to exist side by side with the thrust of present-day physics where possibilities are more important than the events which encase them. From these possibilities, a glimmer of perception will sometimes emerge.

> Each of us advances into his own labyrinth.
> The gift of invisibility
> Has been granted to all but the gods, so we say such
>   things,
> Filling the road up with colors, faces,
> Tender speeches, until they feed us to the truth.

LUCILLE CLIFTON: "I AM A BLACK WOMAN POET, AND I WRITE LIKE ONE" (1936–)

During the 1960s, the Census Bureau in Washington, D.C., received this poignant request from a black woman:

> I was born in 1895, the onliest child of Jace White and Lue Etta Johnson, Fort Necessity, Franklin Parish, Louisiana, baptisted in the Morningside Baptist Church that has a creek running through the grave yard. My folks died when I was small I knows their names because I read them in the Bible. I moved in with some other folks they worked for Mr. Bonner on his farm wasn't no address. They was so many children at that house, I didn't think a soul knew about me and now they tell me that you came and counted. Enclosed six dollars can I have two copies, one for the Retirements, and one for me to show I was there.

In response to the kind of anonymity and human neglect that marks this letter, a number of black women writers have set about with energy, forthrightness, and sometimes anger to assert that *they* have been, and indeed are, "there." Some of these women, such as Alice Walker, Maya Angelou, Gwendolyn Brooks and Nikki Giovanni, have achieved notable reputations, whereas others, no less distinctive in voice, have yet to gain the wider readership they deserve. Among the latter is Lucille Clifton.

In a short prose work, *Generations*, published in 1976, Clifton creates her own "Census Bureau," which, in turn, is a validation of the need for family identity. The book recalls ancestors such as her grandmother Caroline, who came from Dahomey, a republic of western Africa.

> "Walking from New Orleans to Virginia," Daddy would say, "you go through Mississippi, Alabama, Georgia, South Carolina and North Carolina. And that's the walk Mammy Ca'line took when she was eight years old. She was born among the Dahomey people in 1822, Lue. Among the Dahomey people, and she use to always say 'Get what you want, you from Dahomey women'..."

Only through families, the book implies, can we find a true sense of ourselves and how we fit into a larger world. And though family relationships can cause much pain, Clifton suggests that they can also heal.

> And I could tell you about some things we been through, some awful ones, some wonderful, but I know the things that make us are more than that, our lives are more than the days in them, our lives are our line and we go on. I type that and I swear I can see Ca'line standing in the green of Virginia, in the green of Africa, and I swear she makes no sound but she nods her head and smiles.

Lucille Clifton was born in Depew, New York. At sixteen, she left home for the first time to attend Howard University in Washington, D.C., then transferred to Fredonia State Teachers College. After graduating, she married Fred Clifton and started her own family, that would, in turn, become part of the "generations."

> The generations of Caroline Donald born in Afrika in 1823 and Sam Louis Sale born in America in 1777 are

Lucille
who had a son named
Genie
who had a son named
Samuel
who married
Thelma Moore and the blood became Magic and their
daughter is
Thelma Lucille
who married Fred Clifton and the blood became whole
and
their children are
Sidney
Fredrica
Gillian
Alexia four daughters and
Channing
Graham two sons,
and the line goes on.

From her first book of poetry, *Good Times*, to her more recent collections, Clifton has focused on the grief and laughter that family life inspires:

My Daddy has paid the rent
and the insurance man is gone
and the lights is back on
and my uncle Brud has hit
for one dollar straight
and they is good times
good times
good times

Steering a narrow course between anger and sentimentality, Clifton's poetry has been called graceful and incisive. When asked to describe herself and her work, she says simply, "I am a black woman poet, and I write like one."

MARGARET ATWOOD: WOMAN OF LETTERS
(1939–)

The Canadian writer Margaret Atwood takes the entire province of literature as her rightful territory. Besides eleven volumes of poetry, she has published novels, collections of short stories, television and radio plays, and numerous essays. The poems came first, and helped establish both her personal and national identity. If novels and critical prose hold up a mirror to society, poetry (according to Atwood) provides a sharply focusing lens. "Poetry is the heart of the language," she has said, "the activity through which language is renewed and kept alive."

Born in Ottawa in 1939, Atwood spent part of her early years in the wilderness of Quebec where her father, an entomologist (someone who studies insects), did research for the government. As a result, Atwood was eleven years old before she attended a full year of school. By that time, she had already written several plays, some comic books, and an "unfinished novel about an ant." In high school and college, she concentrated on poetry. The appearance of her first collection, *Double Persephone*, printed by a small Canadian press, went almost unnoticed. Only with the publication of a second book, *The Circle Game*, which won the Governor General's Award for the year's best book of poetry, did she receive a certain amount of national recognition. Critics praised her "confident voice," her intelligence, and, most of all, her "unflinching honesty."

> ...(there are mountains
> inside your skull
> garden and chaos, ocean
> and hurricane; certain
> corners of rooms, portraits
> of great-grandmothers, curtains
> of a particular shade;
> your deserts; your private
> dinosaurs; the first
> woman)...
> (*from* "Against Still Life")

In her next two books—*The Animals in That Country* and, especially, *The Journals of Susanna Moodie*—the wilderness of Atwood's childhood began to surface. The idea for *The Journals of Susanna Moodie* came about accidentally when Atwood stumbled upon a journal that had been written by Susanna Moodie, a young woman who had immigrated with her husband to Canada from England in the nineteenth century. The poems are written to sound as if they come directly from Susanna's mind. "Looking in a Mirror," for example, describes the changes that have occurred during her years in the wilderness.

> It was as if I woke
> after a sleep of seven years
> to find stiff lace, religious
> black rotted
> off by earth and the strong waters...

A number of these poems reflect a conflict between an ever-changing nature and man's artificial, static creations. In Atwood's fifth book, *Power Politics*, however, the conflict boils over into confrontations beweeen men and women:

> If I love you
> is that a fact or a weapon?

By then, Atwood's marriage had dissolved, and her attention focused almost entirely on writing. "I chose being a writer," she said, "because I was very determined, even though it was painful for me; but I'm very glad that I made that decision because the other alternative would have been ultimately much more painful. It's more painful to renounce your gifts or your direction in life than it is to renounce an individual."

With the happiness brought by a subsequent relationship, the particular tension between being a writer or a "woman" seems to have resolved itself—along with unreasonably high expectations.

> ... you are not my doctor
> you are not my cure,
>
> nobody has that
> power, you are merely a fellow/traveller...

The other tension, however—the one between natural change and static forms—remains. Atwood links all creative forces with nature, viewing them as part of the same dynamic. The dynamic is involved with language, with naming:

> A peach in boiling water.
> This is a domestic image.
> Try: soft moon with the rind off...

Language, like nature, is constantly mobile, therefore unpredictable. "There are little constellations of language here and there," Atwood says, "and the meaning of a word changes according to its context in its constellation. The word 'woman' already has changed because of the different constellations that have been made around it. Language changes within our lifetime. As a writer you're part of that process—using an old language, but making new patterns with it. Your choices are numerous."

Within these choices, a Blakean vision sometimes emerges:

> I shook my head. There were no clouds, the
> flowers
> deep red and feathered, shot from among
> the dry stones,
> the air
> was about to tell me
> all kinds of answers.

Margaret Atwood's fiction—notably *Surfacing, Lady Oracle*, and *Life Before Man*—has dealt with many of the same themes as her poetry.

SEAMUS HEANEY: THE POET AS DIVINER (1939–)

Seamus Heaney's poetic vocation began with reading lines from Wordsworth's nineteenth-century epic, *The Prelude*.

> ...and I would stand
> Beneath some rock, listening to sounds that are
> The ghostly language of the ancient earth,
> Or make their dim abode in distant winds.
> Thence did I drink the visionary power.

Implicit in these lines, Heaney says, is a view of poetry "as divination [an inspired presentiment about a thing or event], as revelation of the self to the self, as restoration of culture to itself..." The divination involves two important phenomena: the mystery of nature, and the power of words. Often the two are linked, especially when technique and craft come together. Heaney defines technique as "the first stirring of the mind around a word, a rhythm, an image or a memory to grow towards articulation..." Craft, on the other hand, is "helping the thought find the words." The difference between the two is the difference between "receiving" (when an idea or impulse springs up from the mind) and "making."

Seamus Heaney grew up in County Derry, Northern

Ireland, in a countryside rich with moss, stalks, pods, bogs, and natural springs. In describing this landscape, his words ring with spiky consonants—"squelch and slap/of soggy peat"—which make the tongue feel (and the ear hear and the nose smell) the sensory sensations behind the language. He writes of his childhood:

> I loved the fork of a beech tree at the head of our lane, the close thicket of a boxwood hedge in the front of the house, the soft, collapsing, pile of hay in a back corner of the byre, but especially I spent time in the throat of an old willow tree at the end of the farmyard. It was a hollow tree, with gnarled, spreading roots, a soft, perishing bark and a pithy inside. Its mouth was like the fat and solid opening in a horse's collar, and, once you squeezed in through it, you were at the heart of a different life...

"The different life" was the life of a diviner (a person who locates water with a divining stick)—or, speaking figuratively, someone who has willed himself or herself to look for the hidden source of things and release it.

THE DIVINER

Cut from the green hedge a forked hazel stick
That he held tight by the arms of the V:
Circling the terrain, hunting the pluck
Of water...

After college, Heaney lectured at Queen's University in Belfast, and later returned there as an English instructor. It was during these years that his first collection, *Death of a Naturalist*, appeared. The last poem in the book, "Personal Helicon," concerns his obsession with water and describes his youthful terror of peering into a deep well, Narcissus-like, trying to see his own image. Now, he says, his self-examination comes through writing:

I rhyme
To see myself, to set the darkness rolling.

His second book, *Door Into the Dark*, focuses on words themselves as doors into a deeper perception. He speaks of processes—roof-thatching, fishing, blacksmithing—which go beyond the physical "doing" into a new awareness:

All I know is a door into the dark...
The anvil must be somewhere in the centre,
Set there immovable: an altar
Where he expends himself in shape and music...

Between the end of Heaney's second major book, and the beginning of his third, *Wintering Out*, a significant change took place in his work. He attributes the change to two things: his committing himself entirely to poetry, and the effect of a book called *The Bog People*, by P.V. Glob. *The Bog People* is about the discovery, in the bogs of Jutland, of the preserved bodies of men and women from ancient times. The evidence suggests that their heads were cut off as ritual sacrifices to Mother Earth, the goddess of the ground. Reading *The Bog People* reminded Heaney that both the ground of his childhood and the life around him were "charged with significance." In a poem named for "The Tollund Man," one of the sacrificial victims, he writes,

Something of his sad freedom
As he rode the tumbril
Should come to me, driving,
Saying the names

Tollund, Grauballe, Nebelgard,
Watching the pointing hands
Of country people,
Not knowing their tongue...

Many of these poems were written between 1969 and 1973, a time when Northern Ireland had turned violent. This violence is reflected in lines that have moved away from childhood memories to confront a harsher, adult world.

> Is there a life before death? That's chalked up on a wall
> downtown.

Heaney's next book, *Field Work*, gained him an even wider reputation. He began to leave Ireland for frequent intervals of lecturing in the United States, intervals which account for poems called "Leavings" and "Homecomings," and for others that recall home with the mention of "blackbirds" or "sally trees" or "waggons full of big-eyed cattle."

With *Station Island*, published in 1985, Heaney returns to an emphasis on place, but this time the places are archetypal with their echoes of a past when landscape implied "a system of reality beyond the visible realities." Landscape also implies the technique of divination, and in "A Hazel Stick for Catherine Ann," he brings the gift full circle by passing it on to the next generation.

> and the evening I trimmed it for you
> you saw your first glow-worm—
>
> a tiny brightening den lit the eye
> in the blunt cut end of your stick.

SHARON OLDS: "I WILL TELL ABOUT IT"
(1942–)

When Sharon Olds's first book, *Satan Says*, appeared in 1980, there was little doubt that an arresting new voice had arrived on the poetry scene. The main characteristic of this voice was its moral tone of complete integrity. In a poem called "Station," Olds describes the unspoken tension that sometimes develops between husband and wife. She hearkens back to a time when peasants were arrested or punished for poaching, or killing game on someone else's property. Words such as "elegant hand," "beard," "grandee" (a Spanish nobleman), "lord," "archer's bow" act as subtle reminders of those ancient times:

STATION

Coming off the dock after writing,
I approached the house,
and saw your long grandee face
in the light of a lamp with a parchment shade
the color of flame.

An elegant hand on your beard. Your tapered
eyes found me on the lawn. You looked
as the lord looks down from a narrow window
and you are descended from lords. Calmly, with no
hint of shyness, you examined me,

the wife who runs out on the dock to write
as soon as one child is in bed,
leaving the other to you.

>Your long
mouth, flexible as an archer's bow,
did not curve. We spent a long moment
in the truth of our situation, the poems
heavy as poached game hanging from my hands.

Satan Says won the San Francisco Poetry Center Award—an honor especially important since Sharon Olds grew up in the San Francisco Bay area. She first became interested in poetry in high school. She particularly liked Shakespeare, Walt Whitman, Dylan Thomas, and Edna St. Vincent Millay. After attending Stanford University, she traveled to New York to study at Columbia. She is now director of the Graduate Writing Program at New York University, and teaches a poetry workshop at Goldwater Hospital, a public New York City hospital for the severely physically disabled.

Her second book, *The Dead and the Living* (winner of the Academy of American Poets Lamont Award and the National Book Critics Circle Award), established her firmly as a poet of distinction. Although Olds doesn't discuss her private life, many of these poems—such as "My Father's Snoring"—hint at a difficult childhood. With *The Gold Cell,* her third book, the hints become even stronger. In "I Go Back to May 1937," for instance, she invokes the picture of a mother and father standing "at the formal gates of their colleges" about to get married. "Stop, don't do it," she wants to shout at them, "you are going to do bad things to children... " But instead she ends up saying, "Do what you are going to do, and I will tell about it." Her "telling," however, is more than mere accusation; it attempts to understand and identify with their pain.

At the opposite end of the spectrum, Sharon Olds's poems about children involve a different kind of "telling," one of pride and possibility:

> When love comes to me and says
> What do you know, I say This girl, this boy.

One more aspect of Olds's work deserves attention: her ability to empathize with incidents often trivialized by the mass media. One such poem focuses on the abandonment of a newborn baby, who is rescued and brought back from near-death:

> I am
> full of joy to see your new face among us,
> Lee Frank Merklin Jennings I am
> standing here in dumb American praise for your life.

Another poem concerns a teenage girl who, after witnessing the brutal murder of her friend, tries to adjust to a "normal" life.

> She knows
> what all of us want never to know
> and she does a cartwheel, the splits, she shakes the
> shredded pom-poms in her fists.

"Sometimes a story you hear about someone else's life," Olds says, "lodges in you almost as deeply as something from your own experience—it gets stuck in your mind, you cannot stop thinking about it. Writing a poem 'about' that, or 'for' that person is a way of putting down the burden of that thought. At the same time, you're playing in the field of language, you're dancing in language. I feel the energy of language in a poem—a poem that works—as a kind of American Sign Language of the whole body, a kind of rock dance."

Olds doesn't think it's worthwhile to dwell on the issue

of autobiography. "The important thing to us, as readers, is that a poem feels alive somehow, if it dances and we can dance with it." She doesn't discuss her own life because "I want to keep the lives safe from the poems, and the poems safe from the lives." But when high school and college poets ask her what she thinks they should write about, she quotes the poet Muriel Rukeyser: "Write about what burns in you, what you can't forget." And Olds often quotes the statement in the newly discovered Gnostic Gospels, "heretical" parts of the Bible long suppressed: "If you do not bring forth that which is within you, that which is within you will destroy you. If you bring forth that which is within you, that which is within you will save you."

"Each one of us has something different inside. Our job as poets, our luck, our pleasure, is to bring it forth—not just to 'tell about it,' but to embody it, somehow, on the page."

Suzi Mee (signature)

ABOUT THE AUTHOR

From 1975 to 1985 Suzi Mee worked with Teachers & Writers Collaborative and New York State Poets in the Schools, teaching poetry to students in the New York area. She has written essays about poets for *Harvard* Magazine, *American Poetry Review*, and *Literary Cavalcade*. Her own poetry has been included in several major anthologies.

PHOTOGRAPHY CREDITS